SHEEP

FARM ANIMAL DISCOVERY LIBRARY

Lynn M. Stone

Rourke Corporation, Inc.
Vero Beach, Florida 32964

PHOTO CREDITS

All photos by the author

ACKNOWLEDGEMENTS

The author thanks the following for assistance in the
preparation of photos for this book: Marion Behling, St. Charles,
Ill.; Dave Heffernan/Blackberry Historical Farm Village, Aurora,
Ill.; Cotswold Farm Park, Guiting Power, England.

LIBRARY OF CONGRESS
Library of Congress Cataloging-in-Publication Data
Stone, Lynn M.
  Sheep / by Lynn M. Stone.

    p. cm. — (Farm animal discovery library)
    Summary: An introduction to the physical characteristics,
habits, natural environment of sheep and their relationship
to humans.
  ISBN 0-86593-038-4
  1. Sheep—Juvenile literature. [1. Sheep.] I. Title.
II. Series: Stone, Lynn M. Farm animal discovery library.
SF375.2.S76   1990
636.3—dc20   89-29870
                            CIP
                            AC

TABLE OF CONTENTS

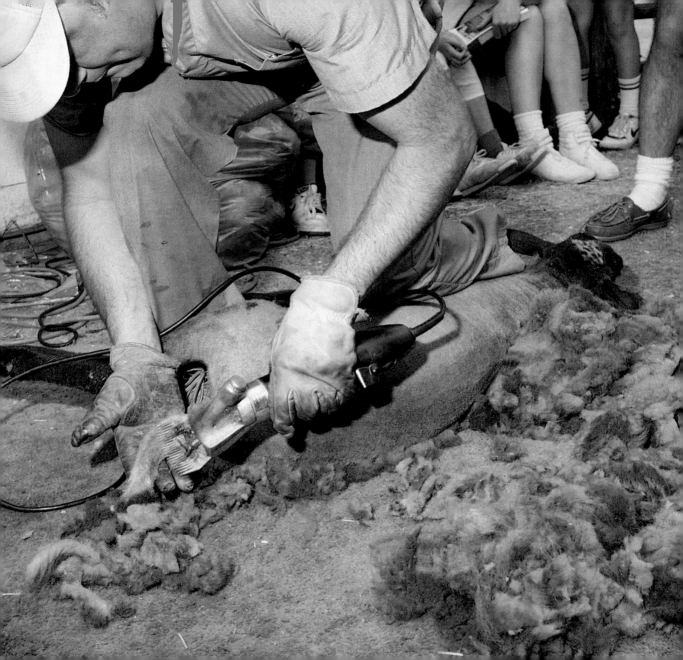

SHEEP

The wooly sheep *(Ovis aries)* is one of the best-known animals in the world. People began to develop tame, or **domestic,** sheep almost 10,000 years ago.

The first domestic sheep in the United States were brought in by European settlers in the 1500's.

Adult male sheep, called **rams,** have often been symbols of power and strength. Baby sheep, or **lambs,** are symbols of love and gentleness.

Farmers raise sheep for meat and wool, or **fleece.**

Sheep are related to goats. Goats, however, have beards, slimmer bodies, and scent glands.

Shearing a sheep

HOW SHEEP LOOK

Sheep are plump, medium-sized animals with two sharp toes, called hoofs, on each foot. When their warm, wool coats are thickest, sheep look much larger than they really are.

Female sheep, known as **ewes,** weigh between 100 and 225 pounds. Rams weigh from 150 to 350 pounds.

In some types of sheeps, both rams and ewes grow horns.

Most sheep have coats of white or a shade of white. Some types, however, have gray, black, brown, or spotted coats.

Merino ewes

WHERE SHEEP LIVE

Domestic sheep live throughout most of the world. Sheep are raised from Iceland to Australia. Sheep on the Falkland Islands are on the doorstep of Antartica, the frozen continent.

Large **flocks** of sheep need plenty of open ground for grazing. All ten of the largest sheep-producing states in the United States are west of the Mississippi River. Texas has the largest number of sheep, almost two million.

The world's largest sheep-producing country is Australia with about 160 million.

Sheep in Yorkshire, England

BREEDS OF SHEEP

Today's farm sheep began long ago with wild sheep as their ancestors. Most domestic sheep came from the wild urial and mouflon sheep.

The 800 different types, or **breeds,** of sheep are all the same basic animal. They differ in their size, horns, and the kind of wool they grow.

Some breeds are raised especially for their meat. Others are more important for their wool.

Merino sheep, for example, are raised for fine, thick, all-white wool.

Orkney rams in England

Merino ram

Merino rams
after shearing

WILD SHEEP

Domestic sheep have seven close relatives living in the wild. The urial, argali, snow sheep, and Asiatic mouflon live in parts of Asia. Europe has a mouflon, and the **bighorn** and Dall sheep live in North America.

The white Dall sheep live in Alaska and western Canada in the mountains. Bighorns live in the mountains and deserts of western North America.

Thousands of bighorns have died from diseases brought to the West by domestic sheep.

Wild bighorn sheep in Montana

BABY SHEEP

Ewes generally have one lamb, but twins are common. Sometimes a ewe produces triplets.

Lambs weigh between four and 18 pounds at birth. Males are larger than females, and some breeds are much heavier than others. The average lamb weighs about nine pounds.

A lamb drinks its mother's milk for three to five months.

Lambs are noisy, often calling loudly, "baaah, baaah."

Sheep usually live for seven or eight years. Rarely, they reach 20.

Ewe and lamb

HOW SHEEP ARE RAISED

Some domestic sheep in North America are raised on small farms. During warm months they graze in fenced pastures. They also eat grain and hay. The sheep have barns or sheds for shelter.

In the Western states, many sheep are raised outdoors on huge pieces of land called ranges. These sheep, in herds of hundreds, live mostly in dry, hilly country.

Sheep dogs help herd the sheep and protect them against coyotes. The sheep graze over many miles.

Sheep grazing

HOW SHEEP ACT

Domestic sheep tend to be shy and helpless. They frighten easily and stay together in a flock. If one sheep does something, however foolish, the other sheep follow.

Rams are not nearly as helpless as ewes and lambs. Rams may try to butt anyone who enters their pasture.

Sheep spend most of their time grazing and resting. Like cows, they chew a **cud.** The cud is food which they have already chewed and swallowed. They simply bring food up into their mouths for a second chewing.

Merino ewe

HOW SHEEP ARE USED

American sheep are generally raised for both meat and wool.

The wool is **sheared**—shaved off—with electric clippers once each year. Shearing is like a haircut.

The wool is collected in the summer when the sheep doesn't need its heavy coat.

The sheep, of course, grow new coats. Meanwhile, the sheared wool is cleaned, dyed, and made into clothes.

East Fresian sheep in Germany are raised for their creamy, protein-rich milk. Roquefort sheep in France produce the milk used in Roquefort cheese.

Glossary

bighorn (BIG horn)—a large-horned wild sheep native to western North America

breed (BREED)—closely related group of animals that came about through man's help; a type of domestic sheep

cud (CUHD)—food which is being chewed after already being swallowed once

domestic (dum ES tik)—tamed and raised by man

ewe (YOU)—female sheep

fleece (FLEESS)—the soft, fuzzy covering on most sheep; wool

flock (FLOK)—a group of sheep

lamb (LAM)—baby sheep

ram (RAM)—male sheep

shear (SHEER)—to remove the wool from a sheep

INDEX